I Finally
Graduated
from
High School

Other Books by Jim

I Went to College and it was okay
I Got a Job and it wasn't that bad
I Made Some Brownies and they were pretty good
I Got Married if you can believe that
I Feel Like a Grown-up Now
The Pretty Good Jim's Journal Treasury

I Finally Graduated from High School

by Jim

dikkers
CARTOON COMPANY

Jim's Journal the comic strip is available at www.gocomics.com/jimsjournal

ISBN: 1499149506
ISBN-13: 978-1499149500

www.dikkers.com

I'm Jim. This is the journal of my day-to-day life.

It actually snowed a little bit while I was in geography class today.

After a while, you couldn't tell if the snow was falling, or the school was rising up.

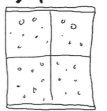

I thought about an alien mother ship abducting the school.

I'll be graduating from high school soon.

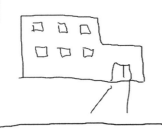

They gave us aptitude tests the other day and we got the results today.

Mine said I would make a good dentist.

I don't think I want to be a dentist, and I felt kind of funny about it all day.

I brought the mail in today.

My mom flipped through the letters really quickly.

Then she said, "Hm..." and walked off.

I tried to flip through the letters like she did and it was really hard.

I shaved today. 	I'm still not quite getting the hang of it. 	My mom walked by and said "It's like having a man in the house!" 	Then she saw all the toilet paper on my face and quietly cleared her throat. 
I met with Mr. Petota today. He's the guidance counselor. 	He said, "So, Jim. What do you want to make of yourself?" 	I told him I hadn't really thought about it. 	He said, "Jim, let's talk man to man." 
Today I looked through boxes of old drawings I made when I was little. 	Some of them were kind of funny. 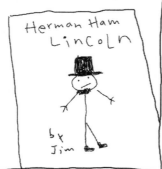	There were old photos, too. 	When I came upstairs I almost couldn't believe three hours had gone by. 

Jim's Journal
by Jim

I watched all six Star Wars movies today.

(I think I drifted off during the Phantom Menace.)

I watched the original Star Wars this morning.

Then I moved on to the Empire Strikes Back.

Somewhere around there I thought maybe I'd watch all six of them.

It felt like it would sort of be an accomplishment.

At some point it occurred to me that Luke was probably the same age as me.

But he fought aliens, had a lot of adventures...

...defeated a whole empire.

After that, watching all the Star Wars movies didn't feel like such an accomplishment.

At school today I had a hard time paying attention.

Mrs. Severt was talking about "The Catcher in the Rye."

She said it used stream-of-consciousness narration and symbolism.

Outside, a bird was trying to fly off with a stick, but it was too heavy.

My mom was looking at samples of cloth tonight.

"I'm making new curtains for your room," she said.

I told her I didn't like any of the patterns too much.

She said, "Aren't you moving out?"

They were having armwrestling matches in study hall today.

Actually, the bigger guys were just threatening everybody else.

"Come on, ladies!" one guy said.

My friends Dave, Hap and I tried to keep out of it as best we could.

"I will not miss high school," Hap said.

I met again today with Mr. Petota, the guidance counselor.

He asked if I was any closer to deciding what I was doing after high school.

I told him I was still thinking about it.

He just stared at me and said, "Tick tock tick tock."

I walked home from school with Sue today.

She's in my English Lit class.

She said, "Mrs. Severt is funny, don't you think?"

I said yes.

Mom said she had a surprise for me when I got home today.

It was a big orange cat. It was sitting on my bed.

"I'm going to need company after you move out," she said.

Jim's Journal
by Jim

My mom was in kind of a bad mood today.

"I suppose I should get a card for my mother," she said. "What a hassle!"

My mom doesn't like Mother's Day.

Today she said, "I'm like the Grinch only for Mother's Day."

Then she laughed.

"It's just a made up holiday," she said.

"Made up by the greeting card companies."

"So they can get their greedy mitts on my four dollars."

Then she left for the Hallmark store to buy a card for her mother.

We have a new cat. His name is Fred.

He used to belong to our neighbor, Mrs. Heggestad.

All Fred does so far is eat and lie around.

Today at lunch Sue and her friend Beth came up to me.

Beth asked, "Jim, are you and Sue going out?"

Both Sue and I said "I don't really know" at the same time.

We all laughed, but it was also really awkward.

I sit next to Mark in study hall. He's joining the Marines when he graduates.

He already shaved his head for it. "I couldn't wait," he said.

He etched a Marines logo in his desk today.

He asked me how it looked and I said it looked pretty good, even though it was just okay.

Mrs. Severt knows I'm keeping a journal.

Today she said, "If you let me see it, I'll give you extra credit."

I said I didn't really want to.

"Quite right," she said. "Quite right."

I drove out to visit my dad today.

(He lives about an hour from my mom.)

"Well, how are you doing, Jim?" he asked.

I told him I was doing fine.

Today my dad asked if I was going to college.

I told him I didn't really know.

He said, "The G.I. bill paid for my college."

That night I dreamed I was in battle, and Mark from school was there.

My mom was getting ready to go to an important meeting today.

She said, "This is the dean of the whole department, so..."

She had perfume and a fancy dress on.

She wrote down a list of things she wanted me to do today.

- pick up mail
- feed cat (no soft!)
- Buy tihfoil & cheese

They had a desk in the cafeteria today for class rings.

They had lots of designs, with names like Vanguard, Integrity and Magnum.

They cost around 300 dollars.

I decided not to get a class ring.

Today I thought about how every atom could be its own universe.

If you go small enough.

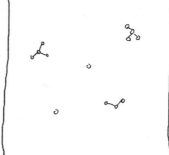

And how our universe could be an atom in a bigger universe.

I'm not sure what I would do differently if either thing were true.

14

A bunch of us went to Dairy Queen last night.

Hap put french fries in his mouth to look like fangs.

It was pretty stupid, but we all laughed so hard that Dave spilled his soda.

The manager told us that if we couldn't be serious we'd have to leave Dairy Queen.

I went to Sue's house after school today.

Her dad was there.

He shook my hand with a really firm grip.

"Jim, are you self-actualized?" he said.

Dave and Hap and I went driving tonight in my mom's car.

It's a Toyota Camry.

"Maybe we'll meet some girls," Hap said.

"I somehow doubt it." Dave said.

Jim's Journal
by Jim

I hung out at my friend Dave's house today.

His house has a distinct "Dave's House" smell.

I'm not sure where the "Dave's House" smell comes from.

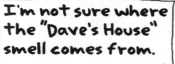

Today I tried to figure it out.

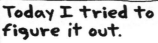

I decided it was a combination of things:

His dad's pipe.

His sister's pet rabbits.

The tuna casserole his mom makes.

And the carpet in their living room and hallway, which is the same carpet they've had since Dave was a kid.

Today I went to school.

It was the last week of high school, so everybody was kind of excited.

One guy stood on a chair and yelled, "the end is nigh!" and people laughed.

My friend Dave said, "Jim, what am I going to do with my life?"

I went to my friend Dave's house today after school.

We played video games and ate pizza all night.

Whenever he got killed, he would say "Oh, the injustice!"

They passed out the yearbooks at school today.

The first thing everyone did was look at their photo.

And that's what I did too.

I asked some people to sign my yearbook.

They all wrote, "good luck."

| I was looking through my yearbook at home tonight.  | My mom started looking at it, too.  | Then she patted me on the shoulder and walked away.  | "Being popular isn't everything," she said.  |

| Today was the last official day of high school.  | Everybody was excited. Music was playing in the halls and people were milling around like it was summer.  | Dave and Hap watched it all and didn't say much.  | "They're a bunch of troglodytes," Hap said.  |

| Graduation is this weekend.  | My grandma came to visit. She's staying at our house.  | She brought a big kit full of all her medicine.  | "Graduation! Well, I'll be," she said. "Jim, you're getting so old."  |

18

Jim's Journal   by Jim

Today was graduation day.

It was kind of funny to see everybody in their robes.

Everyone's parents and families came to the graduation ceremony.

Hap wasn't there.

The other day he said, "Why should I go? I'm done with high school."

Dave said he kind of agreed.

"It's like voluntarily going back to school for one more day." he said.

We walked up when our names were called and got our diplomas.

At that moment, I realized I had finally graduated.

It felt pretty good.

Today I played basketball with Dave at his house.

He said he's been thinking about getting a job.

"Hap's got it made," he said. "He's making $10 an hour at his uncle's sawmill."

Then he said "Sweet," and the basketball swished right when he said it.

Our cat Freddy slept most of the day.

At one point I saw him move.

He stretched his body as long as it could go.

Then he went right back to sleep.

My friend Hap called today.

He asked if I wanted to hang out later.

I said, "Sure."

He said, "Very well... I must borrow some money."

I went to Hap's house today, where He was borrowing money from his brother.

Oswald graduated a couple of years ago. He lives in the basement.

He was surrounded by a bunch of computers that he built. He built his desk, too.

"Architecture died in the early 20th century," he said.

I went for a bike ride today.

I met up with my friend Dave.

We biked almost 30 miles to a small town that had a little diner.

It surprised us how good the pizzas were.

Last night Dave and I felt too tired to bike home from the small-town diner.

We sat around there and played video games.

It started to get dark, so we decided to head back.

It was cold and our legs were sore but we had a pretty fun time.

Jim's Journal
by Jim

When I got up today I was still really tired.

I poured a bowl of cereal.

Then I noticed we were out of milk.

I went to the grocery store when they first opened to buy more milk.

I was still half asleep.

The people at the store were bustling around.

They were loading boxes.

Stocking shelves.

And doing checkout.

It was hard to imagine being that energetic so early in the morning.

22

I saw Hap's brother Oswald today

I asked him if he worked at his uncle's sawmill like Hap does.

"Ha!" he said. "That would not be worth my time."

"Hap barely gets five hours a week there, and let's just say he's the favored relation"

I started reading "Watership Down" today.

I read 5 or 6 pages before I realized I wasn't reading the actual story.

It was just a preface or something.

My mom decided to start a garden.

The first thing we had to do was buy a shovel.

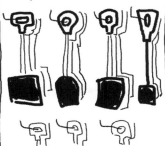

They had all different sizes and shapes.

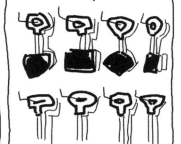

My mom finally said, "Now, that's a shovel!"

I read more of Watership Down today.

It was late afternoon when I finally stopped reading and went outside.

It seemed strange that there was a world outside of Watership Down.

We started work on the garden today.

First, my mom had to decide where in the yard to put it.

She had me spade a patch of grass by the garage.

I worked a long time and hardly made any progress.

Throughout the day, I saw Freddy in 3 different places, but always asleep.

On top of the couch.

On my bed.

And in the laundry basket.

Jim's Journal by Jim

It was a nice day so I decided to read Watership Down outside.

I biked to a field with nice tall grass and a tree.

It was hard to get comfortable against the tree bark.

And I had trouble adjusting my eyes to how bright the pages were in the sun.

Every once in a while a grasshopper would jump on the page in front of me.

I started to think maybe I was better off reading inside.

We haven't planted anything in our garden yet.

My mom looked at seed catalogs all afternoon.

There are like 20 kinds of tomatoes and 15 kinds of beans.

She said, "Gardening is not for the faint of heart!"

Today my friend Sue and I visited her grandparents' farm.

They have honey bees there.

We looked at some of the animals, and Sue picked up a piglet.

"Don't you just love pigs?" Sue said. And I had to admit pigs are pretty great.

Then the piglet started screaming and Sue put it down.

We got the seeds for our garden today.

There was lettuce, tomato and a bunch of other seeds.

I opened some of the packets to look at them.

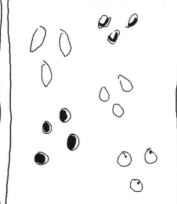

I played basket-ball at Dave's house today.

We don't really play. We just goof around mostly.

Once, Dave tried to shoot a basket from across the street.

He missed.

We ate frozen pizza and played video games till really late.

"I'm doing quite well for myself at the sawmill," Hap said today.

He asked how things were going with me.

I said I guessed they were going okay.

"Are you in any position to loan me 200 dollars?" he asked.

Today Hap told us he's going to make a big action movie this summer.

"Actually, it will be the first of a trilogy," he said.

He told us we would be the stars of the movie.

"Do you know any girls?" he asked.

Jim's Journal
by Jim

Dave and I went for a bike ride today.
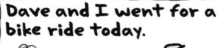

Hap came with.

He kept asking us to slow down.

We decided to bike on some country roads we'd never explored before.

The paved road turned to gravel, then the gravel turned to dirt.

Pretty soon we were in a forest and we couldn't even tell where the road was supposed to be.

"This is a perfect location for the final battle scene in my movie," Hap said.

Eventually we had to carry our bikes out.

Hap stayed behind and called his mom to come and pick him up.

Sue came to visit today.

She showed me brochures for the college she's going to.

"I'm going on a tour in two weeks. I can't wait!"

Then we took a walk.

When I woke up today I heard my mom's piano student practicing scales.

(My mom teaches piano lessons in our house.)

I came out into the kitchen to get a bowl of cereal.

My mom gave me a look like she didn't want me doing that.

My mom went to the grocery store today.

Then she came home and put the groceries away.

She said, "I noticed Mr. Bibbo is looking for baggers. Hint, hint."

She tried to take the last can out of a plastic bag but the bag was sticking to it.

I couldn't sleep last night.

I kept seeing my graduation and Hap's brother and other things.

It was a warm night so I opened the window and looked out for a while.

It was pretty dark. I couldn't see much of anything.

I applied to bag groceries today.

The manager asked if I had any experience.

I told him I didn't.

He said, "Well, I guess I'll take a chance on you."

I called Sue tonight and she wasn't there.

Her mom answered, "Oh, hello, Jim."

We talked for a few minutes about this and that.

I thought it would be awkward, but it actually wasn't too bad.

Jim's Journal
by Jim

Hap shot his movie today.

I played a druid.

I brought Freddy, who was cast as a warrior beast.

Hap brought everybody to the woods to film his climactic battle scene.

Oswald played an evil warlock. He was pretty good in the part.

Hap explained that the trees would come to life and try to kill us.

"This will all happen in post," he said.

But he couldn't make Freddy move, even using tuna.

He tried over and over and got really frustrated. "Freddy, you're the worst actor ever!" he yelled.

Freddy just seemed annoyed that he was there and not lying around at home.

I started at the grocery store today.

I got there early, but by the time I found a smock, I was late.

The manager's name is Dean.

I stocked shelves and Dean said, "That's not how you do it!" and did it himself.

It was really hot today.

I mowed Mrs. Weldd's grass.

She lives next door.

When I was done, she said I could come and visit any time.

I visited Hap's older brother Oswald today.

"Are you going to college?" he asked.

I told him I wasn't sure what I was going to do.

"Go to college," he said.

Some of my friends came into the grocery store today.

They thought I looked pretty funny in a smock.

They pretended to shoplift in front of me.

When they left, Dean said, "Friends of yours?"

I decided to drive out to see my grandparents for the weekend.

It's a long drive.

My mom had a lot of classical music CDs in the car.

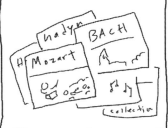

So that's what I listened to.

I arrived at my grandparents' place last night.

They hugged me and said they were glad I came to visit.

Then my grandma said, "We can put you to work on a lot of projects."

Then she listed them.

Jim's Journal by Jim

Today my grandma asked me to pick up a big pile of sticks and old wood in the yard.

She wanted me to move it to a different part of the yard.

My cousin came to my grandma and grandpa's place with his kids.

He brought firecrackers.

We had a bonfire, sat out late, roasted marshmallows and blew off firecrackers.

Grandma and Grandpa were asleep in the house, so it was kind of like we weren't at Grandma and Grandpa's place at all.

My grandparents live in a really small town in the middle of nowhere.

I checked out the local pub by their house today.

Later, Grandma asked where I went and I told her.

She said, "I've lived here 40 years and I have never gone into the pub!"

I left my grandparents' place today.

I thought I could drive back in one day, but I left pretty late.

By 3 o'clock in the morning I still had 100 miles to go to get home.

I was sleepy, so I found a crazy late-night radio talk show that kept me awake.

I worked on my mom's garden today.

It looked like things were growing.

I didn't know if they were weeds or not.

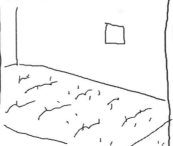

I guess we'll see.

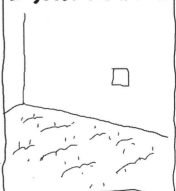

I saw Hap's brother Oswald at the grocery store today. 	He didn't see me. 	I was one isle over when I heard him sigh really loudly. 	He was looking at oatmeal. 
I weeded the garden today. 	It was pretty hard work. 	After a while Freddy came over. 	He didn't know what to make of it. 
Dean had me top the celery today. 	That means cutting the ends off before bagging it. 	There was a lot of celery. 	I smelled like celery all day. 

Jim's Journal
by Jim

I had a really weird dream last night.

I dreamt I was somebody else.

I was some kind of important doctor.

Like the head of a whole hospital.

But I was also like a mafia godfather with a big family.

It seemed real.

Then I woke up and realized I was me.

I was bored today. 	I tinkered with the piano, but I can't really play. 	I walked around outside for a bit. 	I think I even fell asleep on the couch but I'm not sure. 
I heard from the college I applied to. 	They said they were happy to welcome me. 	They said I'm now part of a proud tradition and a member of their family. 	I guess I'll have to buy some new notebooks. 
I walked by an old gas station today. 	There were a lot of rusty old car parts sitting outside. 		I had no idea what some of that stuff was. 

Mrs. Heggestad came over today. 	She wanted to check on Fred. 		She said, "Same old Freddy!" then laughed and laughed. 
It was really hot today. 	I walked by some kids selling lemonade. 	They watched me the whole time. 	So, I went back and bought some. 
I picked a dandelion today. 	I tried to remember that thing where you rub it under your chin. 	I think if your skin turns yellow, it means you like butter. 	For some reason this struck me as really dumb. 

Jim's Journal
by Jim

I don't mind mowing the lawn.

Actually, I kinda like it.

I mowed the lawn today.

The first patch I did, I mowed the outside and worked my way in.

Then I did a patch where I started on one end and worked my way to the other.

And I almost ran over a hose nozzle.

My Uncle Phil came over today.

He has a farm just outside of town.

He looked at our garden and said, "Looks good!"

"You're going to help on my farm this summer."

I hung out with Dave today.

"How did you get two summer jobs?" he asked.

Then he shook his head like he just couldn't believe it.

"You're one of the laziest people I know!" he said.

Hap called today and said "I heard you had two jobs."

He asked if he could borrow some money.

I asked what for.

"Post production," he said.

Today my mom said, "What a waste of a day!"

I bagged groceries all day.

I tried to be careful about what I put on the bottom.

I guess I wasn't doing it right.

Dean said I might be happier somewhere else.

I didn't know if I should go to work today.

It seemed like Dean fired me.

But I wasn't sure.

I walked to the grocery store and just sort of hung around outside for a while. Then I went home.

Jim's Journal
by Jim

bounce bounce bounce bounce bounce bounce bounce bounce bounce bounce bounce

"How is that helping you make the shot?"

It was really hot out today.

Dave and Hap and I shot some baskets at Dave's house.

His mom came out and asked if we wanted to go inside to cool off.

"Going inside is for losers," Dave said.

His mom said, "Well, us losers are going to be nice and comfortable in here."

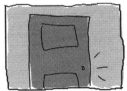

Dave laughed, but I was kind of thinking it would be nice to go inside.

I rode my bike to Uncle Phil's today to help on his farm.

He showed me all around.

I liked the cows.

He said, "Whoa! Time enough for that."

I worked on Uncle Phil's farm again today.

He had me move some hay bales.

It made my hands sore.

He laughed and said, "Your hands are still tender. Give it time."

I was really tired last night.

But Freddy was sleeping right in the middle of my bed.

I lifted him up carefully and placed him at the foot of the bed and he didn't even wake up.

For some reason that struck me as pretty funny.

I worked at the farm today.

Phil pointed out that the corn was nearly six feet tall already.

"Sometimes you can even hear it growing," he said.

I couldn't hear anything.

My mom and I went to the bank today.

We had to arrange my student loan.

I can't believe how much it's going to cost.

They gave me a pen.

We have a rabbit in the garden.

I watched him eat our lettuce this morning.

I suppose I should have chased him away.

But I decided he needed it more.

Jim's Journal   by Jim

"I cast you into darkness... forever!"

"Nooooo!"

Hap had a screening of his movie at his house today.

"The purpose of this sneak preview is to generate buzz," he said.

It took him a while to get his computer working.

He got really frustrated. "It should be playing!" he said.

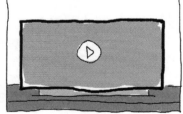

He finally got it to work.

Before it started, he said, "I don't want feedback. I just want applause."

There was an ambulance next door this morning.

I guess Mrs. Weldd is sick

I just saw her the other day when I mowed her lawn.

I wondered what happened to her, but I didn't want to be nosey.

I didn't sleep much last night.

There was a big thunderstorm.

Once, the lightning struck really close.

The next day, Phil said, "That was some storm."

Today we went to see Mrs. Weldd in the hospital.

She has a broken hip, and she had a lot of pills set out.

She said, "We live too long, Jim."

I didn't know what to say about that.

I biked to work on the farm today.

I passed a big dog who tried to chase after me.

I don't know if he was playing around or if he wanted to bite me.

I just figured I should pedal as fast as I could.

Today I biked to the farm again.

And that dog chased after me.

I worked hard all day.

At night I slept like I'd been knocked out cold.

Today I biked to the farm again and raced from the dog.

I worked long and hard all day.

And I had a solid night's sleep.

The days feel like they're melding into each other.

Jim's Journal
by Jim

College orientation is next week. 	I'm going to take the bus there. 	I asked Phil if I could take off from the farm. 	He said, "And so it begins." 
I helped on the farm today. 	Uncle Phil took me to look at his corn. 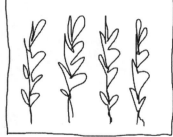	He talked about the seasons and respect for the soil. 	He had me burn some trash. 
I'm taking care of Mrs. Weldd's house. 	She's in a nursing home for a while. 	I have the place to myself. 	I guess she likes spoons. 

I biked to the farm today.

Phil had me clean out the barn.

I hosed down the manure spreader.

Then he gave me an apple.

I ran into Dave today.

He's working on a farm, too, detassling corn.

He takes the tassles off to stop pollination.

He said, "Who knew corn was so scientific?"

I worked at the farm today.

I asked Phil if we should detassle the corn soon.

He laughed and said that's only for seed corn.

He thought I was making a joke.

Jim's Journal   by Jim

"Up next, Jay's weather outlook for today, plus some very lucky ducklings. Stay with us..."

I'm taking care of Mrs. Weldd's place while she's in the nursing home.

She says she'll be back, but I don't know.

She has lots of Reader's Digests.

I guess she likes butterscotch candy, too.

She doesn't have cable. Or a computer.

I wonder if I'll live like this when I'm old.

My mom brought a date home today.

"Donald is an auctioneer," she said.

She asked him to talk really fast. "Oh, come on. Do it just once!"

I really didn't want him to, but he did.

I had to get up really early today.

I took the bus to college orientation.

A student gave us a tour of the campus.

She was really excited about it.

I ran into Mr. Petota today.

He was my guidance counselor in high school.

He said, "You graduated! Call me Sam!"

I never would have guessed his name was Sam.

I fed Freddy this morning, and filled up his water.

That made me think I should water the plants, too.

"Oh, could you water the garden also?" my mom said.

But I thought that was going just a bit too far.

Today Donald was telling a story about a lisping auctioneer.

My mom was listening and laughing out loud at every detail.

"Isn't this just a hoot, Jim?" she said.

At the end of the story she said, "That's what I needed— a good laugh!"

I took Mrs. Weldd's mail to the nursing home for her today.

She had lots of get well cards and lots of junk mail.

She said, "Oh, thank you, Jim," then read every word of the letters out loud.

The junk mail, too.

Jim's Journal
by Jim

Today I decided to read a graphic novel collection of Superman comics starting with the very first issue.

I thought it might be fun.

It started with Superman's father sending him to Earth when his home planet Krypton was destroyed.

I wondered why his father didn't send him to Venus, which seems a lot more like Krypton than Earth.

Krypton   Venus

But I guess that wouldn't have made a very good story.

I'm enjoying my Superman comic.

In the early ones, Superman roughs people up and isn't always so perfect.

He beat up a bad guy pretty seriously one time.

take that!

Donald came in and said, "Superman, huh?"

I worked on the farm today.

I sat at a sweet corn stand by the road all day.

farm fresh CORN

I sold a lot.

farm fresh CORN

People sure seem to like corn.

farm fresh CORN

My mom told me she was going out with Donald tonight.

She was wearing makeup and a fancy dress.

"Don't wait up for me," she said.

I watched Braveheart and ate an entire gallon of chocolate ice cream.

Our garden is doing really well.

We have string beans, tomatoes and lots of other things.

They all taste really good.

I'm getting a little tired of vegetables, though.

My mom asked if I'd go to one of Donald's auctions this weekend.

I said I guess so.

"I think you'll get a real kick out of it," she said.

She said it's for a man who fell and was bankrupted by hospital bills.

Phil gave me 50 dollars today.

He told me I'd been working pretty hard on the farm.

He was especially happy with my work selling sweet corn.

He said, "How'd you like to move up to melons?"

Jim's Journal
by Jim

We went to see Donald work at an auction today.

He was up on a platform, auctioning stuff off, talking really fast.

I reached up to scratch my face once and Don pointed at me and said, "500 do I hear 525, 525, 525?"

Then somebody else raised a hand and the price went up to 525.

My mom said, "You have to be careful, Jim. You almost bought a goat!"

I'm trying to decide what to pack for school.

I sorted out some clothes and stuff.

It didn't look like I was bringing much.

My mom said, "Why don't you take that easy chair?"

Donald was sitting at the table today waiting for my mom.

He told me he actually enjoys waiting around.

"I talk fast for a living, so it's nice to take it slow once in a while."

He laughed, and I smiled to be polite.

I left home for college today. It was about a 5 hour drive.

I got a ride from Brian, a guy I went to school with who has a truck.

I ran into him the other day and found out he was going to the same college.

But beyond that we didn't have much to talk about.

Today was my first day at college. 	I had a big envelope filled with maps and brochures the school sent me. 	I used them to find my way to my dorm, the cafeteria, and other places. 	After walking around all day I went to my dorm room and just sat there. 
I met my room-mate today. His name is Tony. 	He came in our room and said, "Decent, decent," while he looked around. 	He said his brother was in college and told him all about dorms. 	We could've been assigned to places a lot worse than this, Tony said. 
There are a lot of mopeds on campus. 	They zip around everywhere. 	Almost all of them are red. 	I have no idea why that is. 

Jim's Journal
by Jim

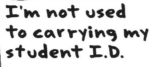
I'm not used to carrying my student I.D.

All I had before was a driver's license and library card.

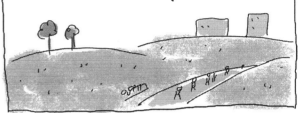

I used to only carry an I.D. when I needed to.

On campus, you need a stuent I.D. to get in almost everywhere.

Today I finally decided to buy a wallet.

It's made of a sort of blue nylon. And it has velcro.

I'm still getting used to sitting on it.

Some guy left all his things by the showers in the dorm.

There was a brush and comb, a nail brush, razor, shaving cream and deodorant.

There were tweezers, tiny scissors, shampoo and conditioner, aftershave, two different kinds of soap, and a special sponge like my mom uses.

He must be a very clean guy.

I got to class early today.

Only one other person was there.

We sat around and waited, but didn't say anything.

Someone pulled the fire alarm in the dorm last night.

We all had to go outside.

The moon looked nice.

Everyone just kept looking back at the dorm, though.

I was walking along the street today.

Someone from a car hollered, "Jim!"

I looked, but I didn't see who it was.

I didn't think I knew anyone here with a car.

Tony and I played video games today.

It was a lot like when I'd play computer games with Dave in high school.

But it seemed less frivolous now, somehow.

Maybe because this was college.

I have to study for a quiz this weekend.

I used a highlighter on my textbook.

When I was done, almost everything was highlighted.

I don't think I'm going to do very well on this quiz.

Jim's Journal
by Jim

I had some visitors this weekend.

My mom drove down to see me yesterday.

She brought Donald.

I gave them a tour of campus.

Donald wore a coat and tie the whole time.

I don't think Don went to college, but I didn't ask.

When we were done, they took me out to dinner.

Donald told a lot of stories and jokes.

My mom rolled her eyes a lot and wasn't laughing.

I felt really energetic today.

I was going to ride my bike but I have a flat tire.

I don't know where to get it filled here.

So, I watched TV all day.

I got an exam back today.

I got a B minus.

On the top of the exam, the TA wrote, "!!!!"

I didn't know if that was good or bad.

I took a walk around campus last night.

I saw a couple people from one of my classes.

But they didn't recognize me.

Tony's right. He's always saying I need to get out and meet people.

I decided a job is a good way to meet some new people.

I went to McDonald's and filled out an application.

I was hired right away and a guy showed me how to put fries in their little bags.

His name was Mark or Matt or something like that.

I worked all day. I must've bagged a million fries.

Today I told my roommate Tony I got a job at McDonald's.

He said, "Ha!"

Then he got serious and said, "Wait—this is no laughing matter."

"You could be my ticket to a lifetime of free filet o' fishes!"

I had a meeting with a teaching assistant today.

She wants to meet with everyone in the class at least once, she said.

I didn't know what she wanted to talk about.

She kept calling me James, but I didn't say anything.

Jim's Journal
by Jim

I get up really early to work nowadays.

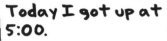

Today I got up at 5:00.

I punched in at McDonald's at 5:30.

My job is porter, which means I mop the floors.

And clean the bathrooms.

And load boxes from the trucks.

And clean more stuff.

After my shift I ordered a big meal and it was delicious.

67

There was a squirrel in the hallway of my dorm last night.

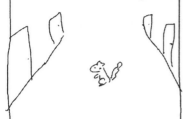

Nobody could catch him.

The house fellow thought somebody brought the squirrel inside, and was pretty upset.

I don't know what ever happened to that squirrel.

I worked at McDonald's this morning.

Then I went to class.

After that I tried to read a book.

But I fell asleep.

I was studying in my dorm room last night.

My roommate Tony was studying, too.

He was also playing a game, chatting, listening to music...

...eating, and tapping his pen on his desk like he was playing drums.

Today Tony said, "It's party time!"

I asked him what party he was going to.

He said he didn't know, but he would find one.

He asked if I knew of any.

It's homecoming this weekend.

It started with a parade. The band was good.

Then there were cheerleaders and alumni officials in new cars from dealers.

It was a pretty poor parade, actually.

I got a letter from a credit card company today.

I have no idea how they got my address.

They said that they wanted to be part of my college future.

The brochure had photos of football players and cheerleaders.

Jim's Journal
by Jim

I took a long walk today.

The campus is bigger than I thought.

I went to the football stadium and got in for free at half time.

There's also an art museum.

And a theater.

On the far end of campus there are cows. For research, I guess.

I asked one of the workers what their names are.

He said they just had numbers.

We're reading "The Great Gatsby" in lit class.

There's a bill-board ad for an optometrist in it.

The professor says it symbolizes God.

When I got home Tony was watching infomercials.

There's a guy who comes into McDonald's every day.

He always orders the filet-o-fish.

But he starts by asking, "What's good today?"

He thinks it's pretty funny.

Tony was upset today.

"I have all these books to read by Monday," he said.

"They call this an education?"

"I'll never get a job reading!"

I need to find somewhere to get a haircut.

Today Tony said, "You should go to my barber!"

He gave me directions.

I said thanks, but I don't think I'll go there.

My mom called today.

She said everything's fine at home.

She really didn't have much to say.

She said I should call more often.

I got a postcard from Uncle Phil today.

I worked on his farm last summer.

He wants me to help again over winter break.

Tony thought that was pretty funny.

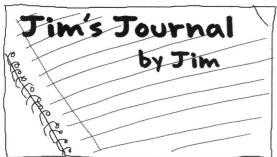

Jim's Journal
by Jim

I've been missing home lately.

In college, everything is pretty different.

No one really knows each other, for one thing.

It's just so big.

People pass each other without even noticing.

I guess that's the way it is from now on.

Steve wants us all to make eye contact with customers.

"Let's make eating here a personal experience," he said.

I made eye contact all day.

It was pretty exhausting.

I dreamt I was on the TV show Lost last night.

One of my professors was Jack, the doctor.

He knew how to get off the island, but wouldn't tell anyone.

Today he gave us a pop quiz.

I spent the afternoon in a coffee shop, studying.

I watched a student protest go by.

I don't know what it was about, but it was nice to see people involved.

It was really cold today.

Tony got a package from his grandma.

It was a new pair of mittens.

"What are the odds?!" he said.

My high school friend Hap called me from home today.

He asked, "How's college going?"

I said I liked it alright.

He said, "So, I guess there's no chance you're moving back?"

I went home today.

It's a long bus ride.

When I got there, a note from my mom said to make myself at home.

She had moved the piano into my room and turned it into a piano-teaching room.

Jim's Journal
by Jim

I'm home for the weekend.

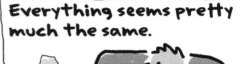

Everything seems pretty much the same.

I went to see Uncle Phil today.

He made a corn maze on his farm.

Kids and families from all over came.

I sold candy apples.

We closed when it got dark.

Afterwards, Phil said "A good day, all in all."

He thinks it's pretty funny that people pay to go in his corn fields.

We're going to dress up for Halloween and hang out downtown.

It's supposed to be a pretty big deal.

I don't know what I'll be.

Actually, Halloween is a lot like college.

My dad texted me today.

He's never done that before.

The message looked like this:

HIJIMNO GWARL!

I called him back.

I ran into Ruth today. She works at McDonald's with me.

She looked different out of uniform.

We'd never talked outside of work before.

We didn't seem to know what to say to each other.

I'm looking at what classes to take next semester.

I really need to take something in science.

Astronomy looks interesting.

I was surprised to see that forestry counts, too.

It was kind of rainy today, but not too bad.

Some people had umbrellas, other people didn't.

I had an umbrella somewhere, but couldn't find it.

When the rain really started coming down, I had to buy one.

Tony told me he didn't sleep at all last night.

"I've never felt so alive!" he said.

He said it was these new herbal supplements he was taking.

"Jim, you should totally try 'em!"

Jim's Journal
by Jim

Our dorm room has been kind of a mess lately.

Today Tony decided to clean.

He played music while he worked.

After a while he opened the window to air out the room.

He put one of his speakers in the window facing out.

I wondered if anybody else wanted to listen to Tony's music

But he didn't seem to care.

Tony ate more of his herbal supplements today.

"I'm taking four times the dose now," he said.

"I can't believe how much energy I have!"

He played video games all night.

Tony slept in today.

I think he slept through all his classes.

When he finally got up he said, "I need more supplements."

Then he couldn't find the bottle and started going nuts.

Tony flushed his herbal supplements down the toilet today.

"I hate these things!" he said.

"If I need a boost I'll buy an energy drink," he said.

"Oh and one other thing?" he said. "They taste like crap!"

My geology professor smacks his lips when he talks.

The lip smacking echoes through the lecture hall.

After class, sometimes I still hear his lip smacking.

But he's nowhere around.

Today I found a place to get my hair cut.

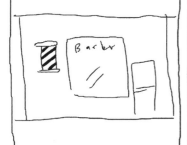

The barber tried to talk to me at first.

But I didn't have much to say.

So he stopped talking to me and just cut my hair.

In lit class today the professor talked about objective correlative.

Authors use it to show emotion without being obvious.

She said writers use objects, events or situations for it.

When we got of class, I went on about my day.

There's a fancy restaurant around the corner from where I live.

Jim's Journal   by Jim

Today I saw families all dressed up, having brunch as I walked by.

There was fruit, croissants, and potatoes.

It looked like a nice place to eat.

I went home and watched "Test Pilot" and ate some cinnamon rolls.

Tony started watching, too.

I asked if he wanted any cinnamon rolls and he said, "No way, that stuff will kill you."

I feel like I'm already getting behind on my reading.

But today I just didn't feel like doing any work.

Tony came in and showed me a foreign coin he found.

It snowed a little last night.

I forgot to bring any gloves from home.

I don't know where to get gloves here.

I guess I'll keep my hands in my pockets a lot.

I was back in my hometown today.

My mom said, "Hi, Jim."

She said Miles Fikema got married, and I didn't know what she was talking about.

Then I remembered that the Fikemas were one of our neighbors.

My cousin's family came over today.

He said, "How's college going, Jim?"

I told him it was going okay.

He said, "Not learning too much, I hope!" then laughed.

Thanksgiving was pretty good.

We have a lot of leftovers.

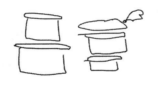

My mom's favorite was the lime Jello my cousin brought.

I got the wishbone, but I didn't know what to wish for.

Freddy has a new place where he likes to sleep.

It's a box with an old sweater on top of it in my mom's closet.

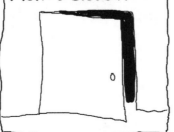

Today I went to look at him.

He sighed when I opened the door, but he didn't open his eyes.

There was a fire truck outside our dorm today.

It was there a long time.

We kept checking out the window to see.

Tony took a lot of photos.

I mopped at work today.

When I got home, I noticed our floors were really dirty.

But I didn't want to mop them.

Tony went to a football game today.

"It's gonna be on TV," he said.

"Be sure to look for me, Jim!"

But I didn't watch it.

I worked at McDonald's today. 	Steve seemed really quiet. 	Some people were saying, "I wonder what's wrong with Steve?" 	But nobody asked him. 
I went to the library to read today. 	I made a note of something and got deja vu. 	I remember hearing once what causes deja vu. 	But I couldn't remember what it was. 
I decided to go to a movie today. 	The one I wanted to see was sold out. 	There was nothing else I wanted to see. 	I didn't know what to do then. 

Jim's Journal
by Jim

"Jim, I've been thinking...."

"I need to exercise more."

"And so do you."

Tony went for a run today.

He asked me to come with.

I figured why not.

I thought it was too cold to be out running.

But Tony never mentioned that.

And he did a lot of talking.

He talked pretty much the whole time.

I sat in a diner today, reading.

They were playing Christmas music.

I'm usually pretty annoyed by Christmas music everywhere.

But this time I was actually enjoying it.

Today was the final exam for geology.

When I first started this class I thought it would be boring.

It turned out to be really interesting at first.

But eventually it got boring, just like I thought.

I took the bus back home tonight.

It was snowing really hard.

In the headlights, the snowflakes looked like stars going by.

Jim's Journal
by Jim

"Hey, Jim's mom. How are you?"

"Real good, Dave."

My friend Dave came over today.

He told me he helped my mom around the house while I was away.

My mom never mentioned it.

"I just never thought of it," she said.

Dave asked me if I was doing his work while I was home.

I told him I was shoveling and stuff like that.

"You've put me out of a job!"

I told him that I felt kind of wierd about all of this.

I looked through the newspaper today.

I feel like I don't know what's going on in the world.

My mom said, "Oh, Jim, you should stay on top of current events."

She took a special "Life After Retirement" section and looked through it.

I saw Sue today.

She was dressed in a festive Christmas-themed sweater.

She said it was for a family Christmas photo.

I couldn't really concentrate on what she was saying because of that sweater.

My grandma made more fudge.

I've been eating a lot of it.

Today I was sick of it.

But I kept eating it.

Jim's Journal

by Jim

My mom doesn't like to celebrate Christmas.

"But Grandma likes it, so I got this goofy little tree," she said.

I got a train for Christmas once.

I think I was about 6 or 7.

I loved that train.

I'd watch it go around the loop for hours.

It would just go around and around, never arriving.

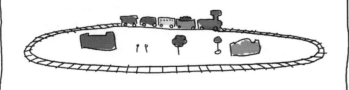

I wonder what ever happened to that train.

Today I had fudge for breakfast.

My mom said, "Oh, Jim, that's too much."

I told her I couldn't help it.

My grandma said maybe she wouldn't make fudge next year.

Today my grandma and my mom went out to lunch.

I stayed home and sat around.

We were all out of fudge.

I was actually kind of happy about that.

I brushed Freddy today.

He normally stands up and turns around when I do that.

But this time he pretty much stayed asleep the whole time.

He just flipped over once or twice.

Sue wanted to do something special for New Year's Eve. 	So we went into the city, drove around and looked at the lights. 	It was snowing a little bit. 	She got out and danced in the snow and said, "Come on, Jim!" 
My mom wanted to clean out the laundry room today. 	"This basement is out of control," she said. 	I cleaned behind the washing machine. 	My mom could hardly believe how much lint I found. 
Dave came over today. 	He asked if he could take any work off my hands and help out my mom. 	"You could out-source to me!" he said. 	I told him I'd be happy to, but that I couldn't afford him. 

Jim's Journal
by Jim

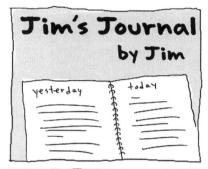

My mom converted my room into a piano studio.

I've been sleeping on an air mattress.

It's kind of fun.

Today I got up really late.

I could smell a big breakfast cooking.

And I could hear my mom and grandma talking about Donald.

As I was walking out, my mom said, "Frankly, I was getting tired of all his jokes!"

When my grandma saw me, she said "Ssh" silently to my mom.

"Oh mother, don't be silly," my mom said. "Jim knows all about it."

I watched a documentary about leopards today.

While it was on, Freddy walked into the living room and sat in front of the tv.

A leopard in the documentary yowled.

Freddy's ears moved back a bit, but otherwise he didn't seem to care about the leopard.

I took out the trash today.

Dave came over while I was putting the bags in the garage.

"Good job, Jim," he said.

Then he started giving me tips for how to do it better.

I got up at 2:30 today.

When I first saw the clock, I didn't know if I was waking up at night or from a nap.

I thought it was pretty amazing that I didn't know.

But soon enough I remembered that it was a nap.

Jim's Journal   by Jim

My mom has a lot of books.

I felt like reading a book today.

I found one about Mussolini on my mom's shelf.

I couldn't really get into it.

Then I found a coffee-table book with pictures of flower gardens.

Great Gardens

I couldn't get into that one either.

Then I found a book of short stories by Franz Kafka.

That one suited me just perfectly.

Today my mom asked me if she should hire my friend Dave again.

I didn't know what to say.

"He does an okay job, but I want someone smart," she said.

Now the whole situation was more awkward than ever.

Today my mom said it would be nice if I brought something to Mrs. Weldd at the nursing home.

I brought a spice cake.

Mrs. Weldd seemed very happy to see me.

She wanted me to tell her all about college.

I noticed some little holes in the snow today.

I couldn't think of what they could be.

I thought maybe rabbits, or squirrels, but the holes were too prefectly spaced.

Then I saw that they were right on top of a manhole cover and it all made sense.

| It snowed today.  | I like the crunching sound snow makes when you walk on it.  | I guess those holes in the snow I saw yesterday are filled in.  | But I had no way to know because I forgot where I was when I saw them.  |

| I went out to get some Hostess Cupcakes today.  | My mom said, "Why don't you bake some cookies?"  | I thought that sounded pretty good.  | Baking them took a long time, and afterwards I wasn't in the mood for cookies anymore.  |

| It snowed some more today.  | I wondered where snow goes when it goes down the chimney.  | I asked my mom.  | She had no idea either.  |

I couldn't catch my breath today.

I'm sure I'm fine. I just wasn't sure what was going on.

I tried a lot, but I could never seem to inhale enough air.

"What's with all the loud breathing?" my mom said.

I had a physical exam today.

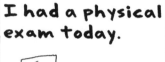

It was just a regular physical.

I told the doctor about trying to catch my breath

He asked if I exercised. I said no.

He told me I was young and it was nothing to worry about.

We took freddy to the vet today.

They couldn't believe how old he was (17), and said he had feline diabetes.

They asked if we wanted to buy the medicine or put him down.

My mom thought about it for a while.

The house seems kind of empty without Freddy in it, even though he was usually asleep.

My mom said, "I feel sort of bad that I don't feel more bad about putting him down."

"But it's not like we knew him. We just inherited him from Mrs. Heggestad."

I felt the same way, but it was still sad because he was such big, sad old cat.

I went to see Mrs. Weldd today.

We didn't talk about much.

When I left she said, "Have fun at college, Jim."

"I hope you have a rich and rewarding life."

I got back to the dorm last night.

Tony was already there.

He said, "So what do you think?"

"It's a goatee!"

Jim's Journal
by Jim

I played ping pong down in the dorm lounge today.

I played with this guy named Sanjay.

He was pretty good.

He laughed a lot, like whenever he missed the ball.

One time the ball hit the ceiling, then a chair, then landed in a plant.

That really cracked him up.

I had philosophy class today.

We're going to learn about a lot of different philosophers, the Professor said.

He seemed really excited about the subject.

None of the students did.

I went back to work at McDonald's today.

Steve seemed relieved to have me back.

"It was rough with all the students gone for a month." he said.

I felt kind of bad for him.

I found a dollar on the street today.

I felt pretty lucky.

Then I looked closely at it and saw that it wasn't a real dollar.

It was some kind of ad.

I worked the late shift at McDonald's tonight.

It was just Mark and me.

Mark worked the Drive-thru and I made the food.

He sighed every time he said "Welcome to McDonald's, may I take your order please?"

Today Tony said he wished he could make food for our whole dorm floor.

"Like a feast of celebration!" he said.

I asked what it would be a celebration of.

He said he didn't know.

We're learning about Plato in philosophy class.

Today we learned about the Platonic ideal.

I had a hard time thinking of my desk as just a shadow of the ideal desk.

It seemed like a perfectly ideal desk just the way it was.

Jim's Journal
by Jim

Unless I get a window seat on the bus, I never know what to look at.

I can't really look out the window, because the person sitting there might think I'm staring.

I hardly ever read on the bus, because whenever I do I get a little woozy.

There's not much to look at in a bus.

Just a couple of ads and public service announcements.

Sometimes I watch the driver.

Usually whoever's driving is pretty grumpy.

But today the driver was whistling to himself, smiling and saying hello to people.

I wonder what happened that made him so happy today.

I bought an enormous cookie today. 	There's a store on campus that sells them. 	Tony saw it and said, "Where'd you get that?" 	So, I told him about the store. 
There's a guy I work with named Sam. 	Today Sam spilled a whole bunch of frozen hamburger patties. 	Steve helped clean them up. 	We had to throw them all away. 
I walked on the train tracks today. 	The rails were kind of slippery and it was hard to balance. 	I noticed some people coming towards me so I walked on the ground for a bit. 	I'm not sure why I was so self-conscious about walking on the tracks. 

Jim's Journal
by Jim

Tony's been putting up a lot of post-it notes.

It seems like wherever I go in our room there's a post-it note.

I didn't say anything about it, but today he said, "Don't mind all the post-its. They improve my life immeasurably."

Sometimes they seem really important.

Sometimes they're kind of personal.

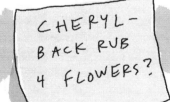

Sometimes they don't make any sense at all.

When I got out of the shower today, one of Tony's post-it notes was on the mirror.

I took it off so I could see, but there was so much condensation that I couldn't put it back.

I didn't know what to do with it.

So I kind of lodged it under the door of the medicine cabinet.

I had to read a book for class today.

I forgot to read it the night before.

I tried to read it while I walked to class.

That didn't work out very well.

I got an enormous cookie again today.

As I was walking into the store, Tony was walking out.

We sort of smiled at each other but didn't say anything.

It was like we bonded over our weakness for enormous cookies.

I saw one of Tony's post-it notes under the dresser today.

There was dust on the sticky part and it was kind of crumpled.

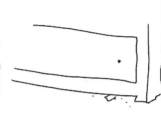

I wasn't sure if it was important.

Tony grabbed it, said "Thank you," and then ran out the door.

I was thinking about mirrors today.

I wonder how they make them.

Is it some kind of special glass? Do they paint it?

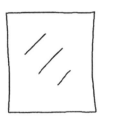

I could look it up, but I didn't feel like it.

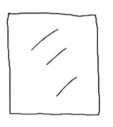

Tony and I got enormous cookies today.

Somebody we know from our dorm saw us.

He said, "Hey, where'd you get those huge cookies?"

We told him all about the store.

I ate a bowl of cereal this morning.

I wasn't really hungry for it.

But I figured I should eat because I knew I'd be hungry later if I didn't.

It was raisin bran.

There's a guy who sits next to me in class who's always cracking his knuckles.

I got an enormous cookie today.

The guy working in the store recognized me and kind of smiled.

It was like he was acknowledging my weakness for enormous cookies.

Maybe I'm eating too many of those things.

Jim's Journal by Jim

We're reading a Raymond Carver book for creative writing class.

It makes me want to be a writer.

Today I went to the library to read, but I didn't really feel like reading.

So I explored the library.

There were big rooms, secret stairs and lots of book shelves.

It was like getting lost in a maze.

And there were so many books I could hardly believe it.

Today I was remembering high school.

How my friend Hap made a movie.

And Dave and I used to shoot baskets after school.

I got so nostalgic I could feel it in my toes.

There's a dog that I walk by on my way to class.

He's always barking.

I wonder what he's barking about.

Our dorm advisor had to fix something about our lock today.

He opened this door that's on our floor that I've never seen opened before.

It looked like a closet or maybe an office.

I don't know why, but I was really curious about what was in there.

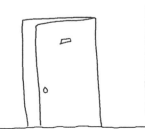

Jim's Journal   by Jim

I had a lot of work to do for school today.

I sat down to write a paper, but then started clearing off and organizing my desk.

Then I cleaned up my room a little bit.

Then I ate.

I really felt like I could use a nap, so I did that, too.

I knew I was running out of time to do my work, but I kept putting it off.

I'm not sure what I'm going to do now.

I was supposed to hand in a paper today but I didn't write it.

It seemed like a lot of other people had trouble with the paper, too.

The professor extended the deadline another week.

I almost couldn't believe my luck.

I worked during the lunch rush at McDonald's today.

A lot of people came in.

I almost couldn't believe how fast I was filling orders.

When it was all over I just had to sit and do nothing for a while.

I went into a pet store today.

I looked at the mice and gerbils and snakes.

It smelled like gerbil food in there, and there was sawdust all over the floor.

Somebody said, "Can I help you find something?"

I said no, then I left.

Today Tony and I moved into new student housing that was bigger than an airport. 	It was so big, Tony almost fell going down the outside stairs.  "Help me, Jim!" he yelled.	Then I woke up and realized it was all a dream. 	It was so obviously a dream that I wondered why I didn't figure that out sooner. 
My roommate Tony made his bed this morning. 	He never makes his bed. 	It was very tidy, with pillows on top and everything. 	I had no idea why he did that. 
I had some cherries for breakfast today. 	They were good. 	I should eat them more often. 	But I probably won't. 

Jim's Journal
by Jim

I walked by a building today and saw something.

I noticed some handwriting on the cement between some bricks.

It was really small.

I could tell it was etched in there when the cement was new.

There's no telling how long ago it was written there.

1990
1982
1971 1964
1950 1942

I imagined a couple snuck onto the construction site and carved their names under the moonlight.

Or something romantic.

117

Some guys in the dorm were hanging out in the lounge last night. 	Tony and I were there. 	They were talking about this and that. 	I didn't say much. 
One of my professors has a funny way of lecturing. 	He looks up, down, sideways, but never directly at the class. 	It's like we're not even there. 	
I wrote a paper last night that was due today. 	I showed it to Mark from my creative writing class. 	He laughed and laughed. 	But it wasn't supposed to be funny. 

My dad called today. 	"I have big news," he said. 	He said he was getting married. 	I told him, "Congratulations." 
I played ping pong in the lounge today with Sanjay. 	He's a guy who lives in my dorm. 	The only time I ever see him is when we're playing ping pong. 	"There's no action anywhere else at this school," he said. 
There was a guy watching Lord of the Rings in the dorm lounge today. 	I saw him when I left for class in the morning. 	When I came back he was still there. 	

Jim's Journal by Jim

Today I waited for the bus for a long time.

There was an ad at the bus stop where I was waiting.

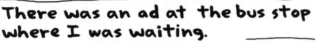

I looked at the ad for a long time.

I took in the lettering, the pictures, the colors, everything.

Whoever made the ad probably never dreamed someone would pay so much attention to it.

But when I got on the bus I forgot all about it.

I couldn't even remember what the ad was for.

That guy who watches Lord of the Rings in the dorm lounge was there again today.

I wonder if he ever goes to class.

When I saw Tony later, he mentioned the guy, too.

"I swear he never goes to class!" he said.

Today at McDonald's Mark seemed more glum than usual.

Afterwards, I walked home with him.

"Steve fired me today," he said.

I almost couldn't believe it.

Mark told me today that he's not too worried about being fired from McDonald's.

He thinks he'll be able to find another job.

"At least, I hope," he said.

"Parental support has not exactly been forthcoming."

Mark came over today.

"Who is that guy?" Tony said.

I told him he worked with me at McDonald's.

We all stayed up late watching Lord of the Rings.

My roommate Tony has a lot of shampoo and soap and stuff.

It takes up a lot of room in our shower.

Every time I take a shower, it seems like there's more stuff.

There's hardly any place for my stuff.

my stuff

I went on the roof of my dorm last night.

There's a ladder on the top floor to a hatch that's unlocked

I looked at the stars for a while.

I wanted to fall asleep up there, but I didn't think that was the best idea.

Jim's Journal
by Jim

Today I was noticing what I see when I close my eyes.

When I close my eyes, here's what I see...

(And I'm not talking about what I see in my mind. I'm talking about what I actually see with my eyes.)

At first it's pretty much just dark.

But then I start to see orange shapes, sort of like a Rorschach test or something.

Then the shapes form into recognizable things.

I see crazy roads and towers, like in a Dr. Seuss book.

When I opened my eyes, Tony was standing there.

He shook his head and said, "Jim, I swear. You are weird!"

I can't remember the last time I rode on a train. 	I like trains. 	There's just something about them. 	I should take a ride on a train somewhere. 
Today I wrote in my journal. 	It struck me as kind of funny that I wrote "today I wrote in my journal" in my journal. 	Maybe I should write "today I wrote in my journal that I wrote in my journal." 	Actually, that's what I just wrote. 
I wore short pants today. 	My roommate Tony said, "Jim, you look positively sporty!" 	I didn't say anything. 	Then he said, "Excellent retort!" 

My dad called me today. 	He said he was getting married on Saturday. 	"You can come," he said, "But I'm guessing you don't want to leave school." 	"Which is fine," he said. 
I bought a Slurpee today. 	I almost never buy drinks like that, but I was thirsty. 	And it looked really good. 	But about half way through I felt sick. 
Today I turned on my lamp and the bulb burned out. 	It kind of popped all of a sudden. 	It actually kind of scared me. 	I don't have any light bulbs so I'm going without light for a while. 

Jim's Journal
by Jim

When I go to the grocery store, I usually just buy one thing at a time.

I'm not one of those people who goes shopping every two weeks and buys a whole bunch of stuff.

Today I was in the cereal aisle when a baby saw me.

The baby stared at me, then smiled.

The mom said, "What do you see? Do you see the man shopping?"

Then the baby started laughing at me.

"Is he a funny man?" she said.

She kept saying in a baby-talk voice, "Is he funny?"

I felt kind of weird about the whole thing so I went to the cheese aisle.

The sun was really bright today for some reason. 	(I noticed I was squinting a lot.) 	I wondered how the sun can be brighter some days. 	I thought maybe it was a lack of clouds, but it must be more complicated than that. 
I decided to make a can of beans today. 	But I couldn't find a can opener. 	I tried to think of some other tool I could use. 	But there was no way to open that can without a can opener. 
At McDonald's today I loaded boxes into the freezer. 	I got pretty cold in there. 	I went to the grill where Sam was and told him how cold I was. 	"How can you be cold," he said. "I'm burning up!" 

I was in a big building on campus today. 	I saw an old painting of a guy. 	I'm guessing he was some kind of past chancellor or something. 	But I could not have cared less. 
I slept in really late today. 	I missed a class and everything. 	Tony told me there was a guy playing drums down the hall. 	Neither of us could believe I slept through that. 
I biked to class today. 	I noticed a lot of different kinds of locks on the bike rack. 	Some bikes were locked up pretty seriously. 	Some bikes weren't locked at all. 

Jim's Journal
by Jim

I sat on a park bench today.

There was a magazine next to me.

Nobody was around, so I figured somebody left it or forgot it.

It looked mildly interesting, so I peered over and read a bit of the cover.

But for some reason I didn't think I should pick it up.

But then I did.

Soon enough I was reading it like it was mine.

I laid in the grass today.

I could see a whole world of dirt and under-grass that I barely notice anymore.

I saw some tiny bugs, and I had no idea what kind of bugs they were.

I did see an ant, though.

Sam invited me to go rock-climbing today.

"It's a major rush," he said. "You should try it."

"Sometimes you get so high you see hawks circling under you."

It didn't sound like something I'd be interested in.

I ate a lot of Nutter Butters today.

I don't know why I ate so many.

It was hard to stop.

Plus they're so small.

Jim's Journal by Jim

I worked the late shift at McDonald's today.

I almost never work the night shift.

I usually work the early shift.

Drunk people came through the drive-thru and held up the line.

honk!

Some crazy guys came in and almost got into a fight.

They knocked over a straw dispenser and I had to pick up all the straws.

I prefer the early shift.

Sam came back from a rock-climbing trip today. 	He showed me a cut he got on his hand. 	"Rope caught me on a belay," he said. 	He said he usually gets some kind of injury every time he goes rock-climbing. 
Today Tony told me he was going rock-climbing. 	"That guy Sam invited me," he said. 	I told him Sam invited me, too, but it was too extreme for me. 	"That's where the fun is, Jim— on the edge!" 
I saw a guy wearing a hat today. 	That made me wonder what kind of hat I'd wear... 	...if I wore hats. 	Nothing I thought of seemed right for me. 

Tony must have some new cologne.

I can smell it all over our place.

When he first puts it on in the morning is when it smells the most.

But even at night, when I'm falling asleep, it's pretty thick in the air.

A guy showed up for class today with a coat, hat and scarf,

even though it was a really hot day.

People asked what he was doing and he said "You never know when the big one's gonna hit!"

I think he was trying to be funny.

I took a good look at the floor of one of my classrooms today.

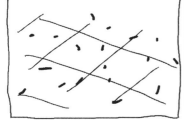

I noticed it was mostly white, but had some colored specks in a random pattern.

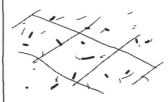

It struck me that this type of floor was a good idea.

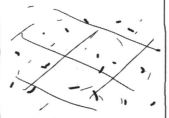

Because when the floor got dirty, the specks would disguise the dirt.

Jim's Journal
by Jim

I saw a lot of acorns today.

I watched a squirrel pick up an acorn.

He held perfectly still, watching me.

Then he ran off.

After a while, he came back, looking for more acorns.

He seemed surprised that there were still a lot of acorns around.

I think he was glad I hadn't taken them all.

Somehow my shoelaces got all mixed up on one foot.

The lace went through the wrong hole on one side.

So every hole below that was wrong, too.

Today I decided to take the time to fix it.

I went to a comic book store with Mark today.

He got talking to the guy who was working there.

They talked about Thor, and how he got his powers.

They were really getting into it.

I just flipped through comics.

I got a postcard from my Dad today.

It was from Acapulco.

It said, "Having a wonderful honeymoon, love you!"

It was pretty strange because he never says "love you."

Today I sat back in my chair and just relaxed.

I didn't watch TV or read or anything.

It was pretty relaxing.

But eventually I got bored.

I passed by a red pipe thing today. I didn't know what it was.

It went from the ground into a building.

It had a meter on it, and a little key on a chain hanging off of it.

I think it might have had something to do with fire safety, but I only thought that because it was red.

I was on the bus today when I saw a bird who couldn't fly.

He was on the grass flopping around.

There was something wrong with his wing, it looked like.

I felt bad for that bird.

Jim's Journal by Jim

I did my laundry today.

There's laundry in the basement of my dorm.

When I put my clothes away, I noticed a penny in the drawer.

I wondered how it got there.

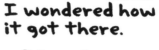

It's not like I put coins in there.

I started thinking about where that penny had come from.

And all the places it's been.

It was a 1982 penny.

I walked home on the train tracks today.	I haven't done that in a while.	I walked on the railroad ties between the rails.	I wonder why they have to put gravel in there.

I looked at the stars for quite a while last night.	I was trying to recognize constellations.	All I could see was the big dipper.	Or maybe it was the little dipper.

I saw Sam today.	He was eating a bucket of popcorn.	I asked if he'd seen a movie or something.	He said no, he was just eating popcorn.

18588288R00080

Made in the USA
Middletown, DE
12 March 2015